HOW TO SURVIVE A
FLOOD

KENNY ABDO

Bolt!
An Imprint of Abdo Zoom
abdopublishing.com

abdopublishing.com

Published by Abdo Zoom, a division of ABDO, P.O. Box 398166, Minneapolis,
Minnesota 55439. Copyright © 2019 by Abdo Consulting Group, Inc. International
copyrights reserved in all countries. No part of this book may be reproduced in any
form without written permission from the publisher. Bolt!™ is a trademark and logo
of Abdo Zoom.

Printed in the United States of America, North Mankato, Minnesota.
052018
092018

Photo Credits: Alamy, Granger Collection, iStock, Shutterstock
Production Contributors: Kenny Abdo, Jennie Forsberg, Grace Hansen
Design Contributors: Dorothy Toth, Neil Klinepier

Library of Congress Control Number: 2017960649

Publisher's Cataloging-in-Publication Data

Names: Abdo, Kenny, author.
Title: How to survive a flood / by Kenny Abdo.
Description: Minneapolis, Minnesota : Abdo Zoom, 2019. | Series: How to survive |
    Includes online resources and index.
Identifiers: ISBN 9781532123252 (lib.bdg.) | ISBN 9781532124235 (ebook) |
    ISBN 9781532124723 (Read-to-me ebook)
Subjects: LCSH: Survival--Juvenile literature. | Floods--Juvenile literature. |
    Emergencies--Planning--Juvenile literature. | Natural disasters--
    Juvenile literature.
Classification: DDC 613.69--dc23

TABLE OF CONTENTS

FLOODS

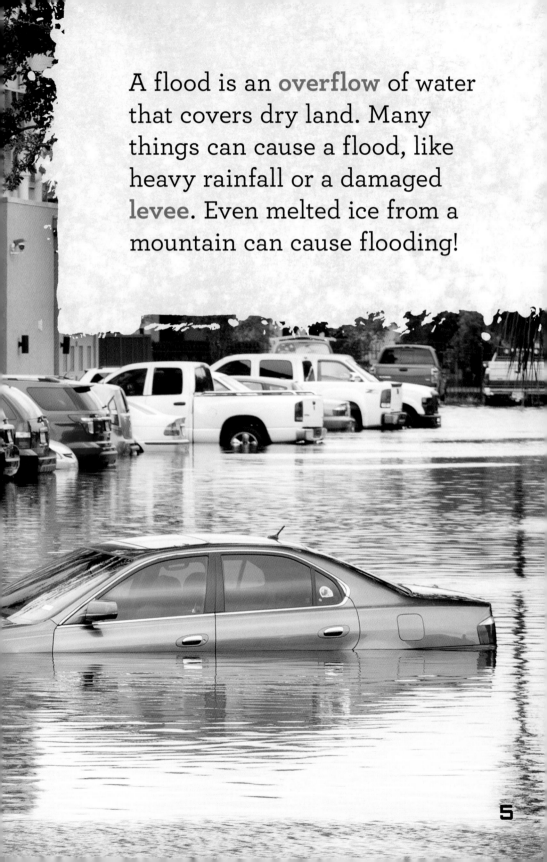

A flood is an **overflow** of water that covers dry land. Many things can cause a flood, like heavy rainfall or a damaged **levee**. Even melted ice from a mountain can cause flooding!

The 1931 Yellow River floods in the Republic of China are one of the deadliest **natural disasters** ever recorded. Millions of people are thought to have died, and millions more lost their homes.

PREPARE

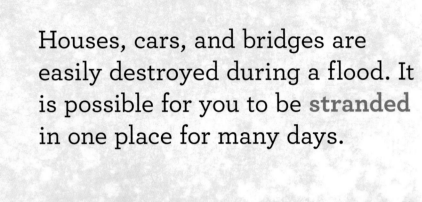

Houses, cars, and bridges are easily destroyed during a flood. It is possible for you to be **stranded** in one place for many days.

It is important to be prepared! You should have a battery-powered radio, extra batteries, and rain gear packed. Medication, bottled water, and **nonperishable** foods can also help you survive.

EMERGENCY PREPARATION CHECKLIST:

Section 1: Emergency Survival Items:

- ☐ Water Containers
- ☐ First Aid Kit
- ☐ Torch
- ☐ Battery Operated Radio
- ☐ Batteries
- ☐ Tinned Food
- ☐ Can Oper
- ☐ Dust

Barriers, like sand bags, can help stop floodwater from entering your home.

SURVIVE

If water rises in your area before you can **evacuate**, move to safety. Safe places during a flood include the top floor, attic, or roof of your home.

If it is possible, turn off the main power switch and close the main gas **valve** in your home. Keep away from downed power lines and any other electrical wires. **Electrocution** is a serious danger in floods.

Listen to your battery-operated radio regularly. It will give you the latest storm information and evacuation plans.

If your car **stalls** in rising water, leave it and climb to higher ground. There you can wait for rescuers to come.

GLOSSARY

barrier – an obstacle that prevents access to somewhere.

electrocution – extreme injury or death by electric shock.

evacuate – the act of leaving or being removed from a place, especially for safety reasons.

levee – a barrier built to prevent overflow of water.

natural disaster – a force of nature that causes major damage or loss of life.

nonperishable – packaged to withstand long-term storage.

overflow – an excess of water.

stall – when a car engine stops running.

stranded – left behind without being able to move from somewhere.

valve – a device that controls the passage of gas through opening and closing it.

ONLINE RESOURCES

Booklinks
NONFICTION NETWORK
FREE! ONLINE NONFICTION RESOURCES

To learn more about surviving a flood, please visit abdobooklinks.com. These links are routinely monitored and updated to provide the most current information available.

INDEX